fifty

kimbell

DR. LEIA BROWN

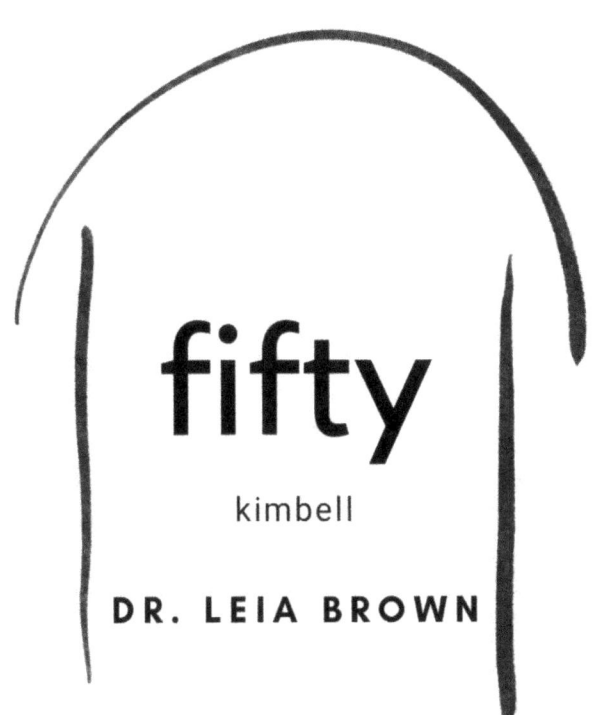

fifty

kimbell

DR. LEIA BROWN

Woman Addressing the Public:
Project for a Monument

Joan Miro, 1980-81

i'm here now, oh, softly straining up
these quiet steps
invisible strings connected like pavement
three hearts strong,
you
like a hole in my chest
you
leaving
just as i arrive
and that's what we had, love:
this timing to collect the art of the ages,
a coming together between
my legs,
arms stretched across America
only to be here,
softly,
next to you

Abstraction

Piet Mondrian, 1939-42

we swore
we wouldn't do this again,
crossing lines
into the blue,
me solid on your horizon
and you like the sea broken against my waves:
straight lines settled in
between sun and sand,
square hearts crushed politely
as the walls caved in
and we
were crushed by the relentless
pursuit
of narrow, of straight:
we swore.

L'Air

Aristide Maillol, 1938

after you
i feel free:
bounding, descending this slope
on lighthearted legs,
my arms thrust out
into yesterday (bent like satirical peaks)
and forward into tomorrow,
elbows exceeding time
while i slide into home,
softly touching your cheek with my fingers
and i recall
before
as if it never existed,
as if i was always
this happy, this frightened
of falling away from you

The Mountain (La Montagne)

Aristide Maillol, 1937

before i touched you
love was a mountain:
i sank down,
hair in hands, reclined
while worlds declined
and you, far away, unkempt as the breath of demons
roared
like fire, casting me into forever,
forged into purgatory,
lifted (as heavy as i was)
and severed from the very mountain
from which i came:
the lonely haul of marble,
sculpted alone
and folded up flat into myself

Weeping Willow

Claude Monet, 1918-19

i saw this one coming,
a blind tree in the darkness:
i swirled branches together
until they slipped knots around my memory
and i swept fear as it crept
in a deluge
underneath rivers,
underneath stones
and you were closed eyes
dreaming in the dark,
me finally screaming
when it came,
bitter walls of sweetness
wrapped around me, a coma of lightness
painted in perfect reverie

Composition

Piet Mondrian, 1914

i remember this neighborhood:
a curve of knowing
as we race around metallic corners
this roof smiles
and that one breaks,
sunlight glinting off windows
as we furrow into edges,
finding home
while the architecture of my heart
fades into sunset
and i follow you
through all these lines,
the rose gold of me
melting
into the asphalt gray
of you

Head

Amedeo Modigliani, 1913

we were never alone:
circles and bones
carved
into caves, the smooth
egg
of my face,
dove grey
and my cheek pressed
softly into yours while you trace outlines
on my hair:
forehead on fire
as my body disappears
into the abyss,
held up only
by the oval
of you

Girls on the Pier

Edvard Munch, 1904

the first time we met
was on a bridge,
me waiting for you
while the moon painted sighs
into skies,
timid reflections
fading purple
as i met myself
on that bridge,
waiting for you
waiting for me
before the hill rose up pink
under the mountain
where we lived
before this town was born

Maison Maria with a View of Chateau Noir

Paul Cezanne, 1895

our home
emerged
from the blank slate of this wilderness
between two trees
wild hearts beating like leaves
as the wind blew us
from dream to dream
down this lane
towards the evergreen slalom
of eternity

On the Pont de l'Europe

Gustavo Caillebotte, 1876-77

we rode trains like triangles,
falling over each other up the hill
and you made me into modernity
shifting wheels with solid walls
me
dragged slowly over bridges,
constantly pointing you
toward the past
until finally
we pulled fishbowls
out of your hat
and we found Europe like
we found each other:
open rolls of hills
waiting
on whimsical roads
for the cast iron notes
of the future

Roe Deer at a Stream

Gustave Courbet, 1868

this is the fright
beside our stream of peace
we wade in uncertainty
like fish
skating past our ankles,
brimming over with sadness,
wrinkling our toes
in water
as it flows
unbothered over rocks
and our pebbles fray
a thousand years at a time,
standing here beside us
inside time, inside calm sprays
of tree branches
and delight
just waiting for sparks
to send us
flying

Glaucus and Scylla

Joseph Mallord William Turner, 1841

i fade into gold,
the softness of you
how you need to hold my hand
to fall asleep
how when i let go
you slide your other hand
into yours,
into the warmth of where i was
to remember me
in the night
as i softly fade away,
as i creep
silently down the liquid hallway
between this room
and the golden fold
of the next

Dog Guarding a Basket of Grapes

Ferdinand Georg Waldmuller, 1836

this is all of us:
alert
to the profound potential
of a possible loss,
so we stand guard
feet wide
heart clenched
eyes locked,
as you creep in
to take away
this treasure i found,
my heart in a basket,
my longingness for you
made solid
in the form of a grape
before we
became wine

The Grand Canal, Venice, Looking Toward the Rialto

Richard Parkes Bonington, 1826

we are sinking
slowly up, a caramel ice cream sky
gelato in our shoes
as we cross bridges,
back and forth
between buildings
we are clouds
rising up
lifting our arms like clothes lines
across the water
waiting for boats
that never come
and yet always
the sound of you
snoring across channels

Portrait of Mary Anne Bloxam (later Mrs. Frederick H. Hemming)

Thomas Lawrence, 1824-25

the thing is
i love you
but i also wonder
how long i will pay
for the sins
of the women
who came
before me, you
ripping buttons
off your shirts
less in lust,
more in anger
and so i wait
for the time
when i can love you
without curtains

Portrait of Frederick H. Hemming

Thomas Lawrence, 1824-25

i wonder
what you have
under your collar:
smug world waiting to strangle you
or proof that you were loved
last night
under sheets
or ways that you have stretched
longing for hope,
lifting your head
out of heavy waters
straining against the constraints
your family pressed
upon you
or struggling silently
to accept mine
for who they are:
i wonder,
and i wait

Ideal Head of a Woman

Antonio Canova, 1817

i close my eyes
and i wonder:
am i everything
you wanted me to be
cold hard beauty
with an aristocratic nose
or cracking under
the polygamous weight
of my perfect hair,
every strand
in place
and i breathe,
i breathe,
a marble bust
with no one's arms
and a tight lipped smile
just waiting
to be held

Portrait of Monsieur G. Giving his Daughter a Geography Lesson

Louis-Leopoldo Boilly, 1812

i can show you the world
(how it shimmers)
but you you you stay here
(it's not safe) and you
will never see it,
the slums of discovery
torn inside out
a dark room and i
rip open wide the curtains
on their casters,
a globe inside a globe
and i can show you everything
and yet
i turn away
from the maps, from my obsession
for you
for you, my darling:
my obsession

Portrait of Miss Anna Ward with Her Dog

Joshua Reynolds, 1787

i waited my whole life
to belong
like this:
this whole worldness of us,
the two of us
out of doors
and yet
we are surrounded
by this, this house
our trust
built up out of our bondage
those years of not belonging
those empties
those flurries of hope
coming out at us
from cages
and then finally, you:
my girl
my world

Portrait of Mrs. Andrew Reid

George Romney, 1780–88

look at me
in my leisure
waiting gently
for my boredom
to coalesce
and i
i am
am so
so very
very happy
my favorite blues,
a garden of bliss
at my feet
and yet
i've been eclipsed
by my own beauty:
swallowed in the lace

Portrait of Janet Anderson

Henry Rayburn, 1780s

you think this is easy
this aging
but all my clothes have memories
and they hold me tight
dying harder
every time i put them on
so this little smile
is not you:
it is twenty years ago
when i first saw your face
and now i hold the part of me that hurts
when i wear this again
and my body begins to reminisce
on when you were young
(i hold your hand
inside my sleeve)
and i hurt

Self-Portrait

Elisabeth Louise Vigee Le Brun, 1781

i hoped you would see me
like this:
wrapped up in bows,
my whole world
in the chalcedony orbs
draped longingly
from my ears
and i dream of you
near me,
wrapped around
like a coat
against the darkness
and me, the light,
those tender imperfections
clipped halfway back
until i can trust
the nearness of you
and wholly release
this half hearted smile

The Fountain

Hubert Robert, 1775-78

it's galadriel for me:
the wind blown elvin longings,
dying trees
falling over
as we gather
against the age,
against the light dying
in your eyes
against the constant
upward motion
of life
slipping through our fingers..
it's the ageless
reaching
for me,
my father soaring
up the steps
to meet me
that brings me
to this place
of otherworldly bliss

Boreal Aducting Oreithyia

Francois Boucher, 1769

there are so many flowers
hidden
in the folds
of this fabric
a baby crying in the kitchen
and i am distracted
by clouds
you coming to take
me away:
every blue meeting every green
the cherubic pink
of the sky
and your wings
enveloping madness
as we go

Lord Grosvenor's Arabian Stallion
with a Groom

George Stubbs, 1765

is this love
(everything underneath
and i wonder
if i had to die
for this portrait,
for you to study me enough
to take me home
to hang me up
on the wall, another trophy)
and yet
this light
claims me,
fields of fire taking over
as trees discover
this folly:
me,
at the end of the day,
owning you

La Simplicite (Simplicity)

Jean-Baptiste Greuze, 1759

the simple truth comes
in waves, petals falling
hats folded like baskets
hearts in half
and me, falling in love
with you
by proxy
as i tip each frond
softly into my lap
blissfully unaware
of my future
as it comes,
storms drifting over horizons,
and me:
young, calm, unbothered,
and free

Portrait of a Woman, Possibly Elizabeth Warren

Joshua Reynolds, 1759

this is later
this is life: the part
where i've grown up
where i stand under urns
waiting for sunset
where you come clean,
holding on
to my hand
while i fall asleep
and it still hurts (the empty)
fingers held up to the sky,
your heart reverberating
in my ears
until nothing matters
but you
and the way my toes curl
inside my shoes

Portrait of a Woman, Possibly of the Lloyd Family

Thomas Gainsborough, 1750

i cannot fathom
a life indoors
this loud, this angry
this soft, this quiet:
me sitting solemnly
in the arms of a tree
moving mountains
with each tilt of my neck
and i would wait for you
for always, while the moon
turns the mountains blue
but you
showed your cards
too soon

Heureux age! Age d'or (Happy Age! Golden Age)

Jean-Antoine Watteau, 1716–20

i could hear them laughing
through the walls
my heels dug in
loathe to let their lithe lights
be my undoing
but
i am bound by
the biological imperative,
the thing that screams hold me
in the night
the laugh that echoes
beyond my dreams
and holds me forever fugitive
in this divine joy
of parenthood

Beauty in a Black Kimono

Tori's Kiyonobu, 1710-20

i hurt -
clutching you,
darling babe in sandal feet
draped discreetly
against
my barren timeless belly,
wrapped asunder
and i rip
silk petals
off pages
while i become paper,
pale silver lack
in hard floral black
and i tip forward -
i hold the pain
in my hair

Pastoral Landscape

Claude Lorrain, 1677

the sky slips away
and we are calm
as sheep,
gathered softly under trees
light dipping
as they come
and we begin to tether ourselves
to each other
in this approaching dawn,
the dank dark brightness
coy in the distance,
splashing atop
water, rocks
crinkling like paper
and we sink,
faster, faster,
into the wild wilderness
of civilization

Rough Sea at a Jetty

Jacob van Ruisdael, 1650s

my stomach rolls
with you
the way this feels
sound breaking like waves
and you silent
staring
at the sea
waiting for me
to materialize,
for the broken grey lines
in my eyes
to dissipate, to wound you
as rain falls, tears
from the sky
boiling night winds
and whipping
them
until i can no longer
stand:
i am at the edge
with you

The Madonna and Child with Saint Martina

Pietro de Cortona, 1645

i won't share this
with you:
my sharp tongue
and finally
my turn
to hold my savior,
to be saved
by the newness
by the freshness
of his skin,
and i refuse to bend
these two memories,
this blonde me before you
reaching for the child
and this motherly me
after you,
wound up in you,
smothered by the fulfillment
of my dreams

Interior of the Buurkerk, Utrecht

Pieter Jansz. Saenredam, 1645

i feel dwarfed
by this
by the magnitude
of the emptiness
of my feelings,
chandeliers of fear
fading into ceilings,
lines drawn
in curves
stretched like fingers
so i sink down,
my back pressed cold
into columns
sitting alone here
on floors,
a checkerboard
a world
away from you

Still Life with a Bowl of Strawberries, Basket of Cherries, and Branch of Gooseberries

Louise Maillon , 1631

the lights went out
while i
was waiting for you,
a basket of newness
branched out
in me
the solid lines of tables
stretched out strong,
your arms
underneath me
and your heart
holding my spirit,
fruit gently resting
in your hands
and gradually
i will unfurl my leaves
for you,
for only you,
in the darkness of the light

Large Jar

Japanese, 17th or 18th Century

this is the beauty:
soft gold flecks
tucked warmly
into my imperfections,
our wounds
now make me stronger
and i
hear music
as you mold me,
as you wrap your hands around me,
as you form me in your womb
on your table
in your heart
and i long for this,
for this betterness made better
by you:
by the filling up of my heart
in your embrace

Evening Landscape

Japanese, c. 1540

i sketch everything
first:
an evening of solace
before i speak
and then the composite need
to gently erase myself
after
each mistake,
drawing me up into you,
covered mountains
at the dawn of time
and me,
alone together
gazing at horizons
they will remember
for eons

Head of a Woman

Sebastiano del Piombo (Sebastino Luciani), early 1530s

this is every woman
in the quiet,
held
softly below you
in the turquoise
wall of the sea,
my hair
wrapped up in
solid tendrils of time
drifting and darkening and holding
me:
hope everywhere
in circles,
carnelian beats
and the timeless beauty
of my face
fading quickly
into
the roundness
of all of us

The Madonna and Child

Parmigianino (Girolamo Francesco Maria Mazzola), 1527-30

your skin:
i can't look at your skin
without my heart breaking
me green,
a barren womb thrust
into instant
motherhood
and you
perfect beyond all reason,
gazing at me:
loving me in ways
i don't deserve
and as you coo
i realize
this coup for what it was:
that i will now spend all of my days
holding you tenderly,
unable to look you directly in the face
for fear
my haloed heart
will break

Fortitude and Unidentified Virtue, Possibly Hope

Bambaia (Agostino Busti), 1520-1525

i stand strong
here
open inside
and holding on,
ready to wrap
my hands around you:
tomorrow
i will be better
i hope, i think,
and able to stand
on my own
for every waking moment
wrapped in my own
fabric: smiling
while
everything lifts
up, up, up

Christ the Redeemer

Attributed to Tullio Lombardo, c. 1500-20

hold me, Lord,
in your glow:
head turned towards the light
amid the softness
and the hardness,
your profile
unending,
carved solid
into my heart
and i remember
those thorns
they threw at us, those
cross words
overflowing
our cups
and i drink
in the solace
of your name

Portrait of Jacob Obrecht

Quinten Metsys, 1496

this is the pious version
of me,
my anger broken
like buttons
and pulsing through my hands,
a closed circuit
of fingers
while i humbly submit
my faults
to your grace
and although my sins
are written in gold
on the wall
they are behind me
as much as
You are

Pink and White Lotus

Chinese, 14th Century

you are flowers
on my wall,
a kitchen tapestry
rolled out
timeless
and stretched,
happy leaves floating
across ageless
water:
mangoes and cream,
the currency of green
smiling
at me
under centuries
of dirt,
wiped clean
and gilded
into hours

Miniature Casket

French, c. 1250-1300

i watch you sleeping
chest rising
star flowers
and i count your breaths
in and out,
out and in,
counting all the ones we lost
when this world ended
for me:
suddenly
i am life
without you
while worlds keep right on blooming,
spinning wild gold circles
into nameless
caskets

Reliquary Arm

French, c. 1150-1200

peace, honey, peace:
i call it
and
i hold it
in my elbows
turning around slowly,
a golden hand
pointing me home
and
i am convicted
by this,
by this defect
in my heart,
by my own deficits
and
i am convinced
this is all you need
to follow me
into
the stardom
of forever

Court Lady

Chinese, 8th Century

i ate quinoa
and i remember
seeing you
in a classroom,
arms floating
above us
while we judged ourselves
for the extra weight
that we carry:
my cheeks red
with shame
and satisfaction,
the happiness of memory
and your
everlasting gaze
wrapped firmly
around me
like gauze

Standing Dignitary

Ancient American, c. 600–1000

ooh i love you:
the quirks
that make you mine,
your straight lines
running into mine,
playful toes
tipped forward
into armless wanting,
faces
happy knowing you,
robot blocks
a century before
we were created
and you,
standing happily
at the door
with poodles at your knee

Peacock and a Flower

Roman, c. 400

how did you last so long:
prolonging me
into distances
navigated by time,
tails furling
with feathered clocks,
flocks ticking
until we become
the flowers
that grew
from our bodies
mosaics of laughter
dripping together,
crowns on my head
as i quietly scream:
i'm gone

Seated Womam

Ancient American, c. 1500–1200 B.C.

yes
it's me
sitting here at your table
not bearing any arms,
no ill will
except for you
and to temper my ruffled fate
i swaddle myself up
inside out
and cross my legs
to plead with you,
to smile
as you reverse my face,
as you grimace
at my inability to rise

Female Figure

Bastis Master, c. 2500-2300 B.C.

we had a fight
this morning and
five thousand years later
this is still how i feel:
arms wrapped up wildly
around this ache,
trying to keep it in,
spinning my grief
in circles
until it breaks
and we are left limbless,
listing in the lull
of the bigness
of time

www.ingramcontent.com/pod-product-compliance
Lightning Source LLC
Chambersburg PA
CBHW071144220526
45467CB00015B/1830